THE MODERN HOUSE

THE MODERN HOUSE

Jonathan Bell, Matt Gibberd & Albert Hill

Artifice
books on architecture

FOREWORD

by

MATT GIBBERD & ALBERT HILL

Founding Directors

We have been selling Britain's most accomplished modern houses and apartments for a decade, and the time seems right to collate our pictorial archive under one suitably modernist roof. The majority of the photographs you see here were commissioned by us for marketing purposes. These are real homes inhabited by real people. Rather than being an exhaustive architectural survey, this book instead offers our own distinctive snapshot of what it means to live in a modern way in Britain. When we started The Modern House, we had little idea of the richness and diversity of our country's modern heritage, a heritage that continues to grow with every audacious new project. We are in the privileged position of being able to visit these buildings, to experience the domestic architectural landscape as it evolves in front of us. The book is a celebration of what we have discovered behind carefully clipped hedgerows and unassuming warehouse doors. We hope it conjures the same sense of excitement that we ourselves have felt.

themodernhouse.net

MODERN LIVING
IN THE NEW ERA

by

JONATHAN BELL

The way we live our lives isn't always reflected by the spaces we live them in. For a hundred years, architects and their clients have strived to create a new domestic paradigm, one that best represents the demands and technologies of the era. The modern house is where architecture and aspiration come together, where the possibilities of new techniques are translated directly into the everyday experience of life. To live in a modern house is to have a greater appreciation for the simple and the everyday, from the movement of the sun to the changing of the seasons, to the texture of a surface or the act of moving through a sequence of spaces.

The modern house is still a rare sight in the built environment. It is nearly 90 years since the first flowerings of modernity, beginning with idiosyncratic outliers like Peter Behrens' New Ways in Northampton and culminating in the first truly 'modern' British house, Amyas Connell's High & Over in Amersham (see p 108), a bold statement that formed a very visible break with the past. Despite the high profile of the houses that were built —and the interest and ire they raised—the aesthetics of the avant-garde remains a niche pursuit, for both architects and clients alike. Yet over time, the impact of these pioneering homes has never dimmed, their detractors have melted away and contemporary design has finally become the most desirable way of building a new home in the modern era.

The evolution of the modern house runs parallel to the evolution of culture and society. The very first contemporary, architect-designed structures were outliers, criticised and derided by the establishment and viewed as a curiosity by the majority of homebuyers. The new villas stood out starkly against their traditional neighbours, occasionally attracting barbed comments from reactionary quarters. Today, those early houses are acclaimed for their audacious forms, radical plans and innovative use of materials. Concrete allowed facade and structure to be closely related, while steel-framed windows allowed huge expanses of glass; architecture, once the most formal of arts, was liberated by the possibility of abstraction.

Britain's role in these early years of the Modern Movement was as a staging post and petri dish. Modernism was not a British invention, but it was in the seaside towns, interwar suburbs and uptown plots that the seeds of the new architecture took root, borne by a wave of pioneering exiles including Walter Gropius, Serge Chermayeff, Erich Mendelsohn,

Marcel Breuer, Berthold Lubetkin and Ernö Goldfinger. The latter two made England their home, but many others passed through the UK on the way to greater success and recognition in the US, leaving behind short-lived but fruitful partnerships. For many years, the houses of the interwar period were considered eccentric diversions, alien in form and character to the tradition of British architecture.

Nevertheless, for all the avant-garde and progressive posturing, many of the aesthetic and material devices used in the new architecture had parallels with much earlier architectural movements. Abstraction and pragmatism, truth to materials and process, a desire to connect architecture with site, surroundings and society; all were inherent qualities of the Arts and Crafts Movement, which in turn built upon a noble interpretation of the master builder. When Hermann Muthesius published his epic and influential illustrated architectural travelogue *Das englische Haus* at the turn of the twentieth century, it served to illustrate the idiosyncrasy and sheer variety of styles of domestic architecture in the country. Muthesius was the progenitor of a new wave of interest in industry and craft, the end destination of which was the Bauhaus.

Britain's experience of the great German design school was second-hand and often lost—or at least substantially altered—in translation. Many émigrés used its tenets in their work in the country, and local firms followed. By the time FRS Yorke had published the first edition of his seminal book *The Modern House* in 1934, there were sufficient admirers, imitators and originals to merit a 14 page section on English examples. This handful of bold experiments included works by Yorke himself and by Val Harding with Tecton, as well as experimental work by Grey Wornum (later to complete the RIBA headquarters in Portland Place) with Richard Sheppard, the founder of Sheppard Robson.

The great irony at the heart of Modernism is how a movement rooted in functionalism could act as a conduit for personality, individuality and expression. Any fears that the 'alien' architecture would be blank, sterile and lifeless were swiftly dispelled. Instead, this book chronicles a wide variety of very different houses, all of which have emerged from a vortex whipped up between the client and architect. Some of the greatest contemporary houses of the twentieth century were the result of bold characters, eccentric demands and vivacious choices, from both sides of

the creative partnership. The populist view of the architect—especially those of the modernist persuasion—was greatly informed by satire and exaggeration, qualities that a largely unselfconscious profession did little to dispel. Evelyn Waugh's portrait of Professor Otto Silenus in *Decline and Fall* (1928) summed up the cliché of the humourless, inhuman functionalist ("The only perfect building must be the factory, because that is built to house machines, not men"). Architects could, of course, be dogmatic and principled, idiosyncratically dressed and eccentrically mannered, but most were also vivacious and genuinely engaged with progressive social, cultural and political attitudes and movements.

The risks taken by bold clients and forthright architects, often in the face of much local opposition, are perhaps the genesis of every house featured in this book. For architects and their clients, the new materials, technologies and aesthetics meant that their house could finally be free from the weight of history, or at least from the perceived strictures of the vernacular. By the end of the first half of the twentieth century, 'traditional' design had degraded into lacklustre pastiches that were replicated in the hundreds of thousands. The new architecture promised new life and freedom, engagement with culture, art, society and progressive values. It spoke of a future world of prosperity and health delivered by technology and efficiency, yet at no point was personality and humanism dismissed.

It is futile to speculate how Britain's domestic architecture might have evolved in the absence of an all-consuming global war. The immediate halt of construction, and the departure and death of many architects, didn't extinguish the dream of progressive design, and architecture emerged as a potent force in the post-war world, an instrument for change through vital reconstruction. Although Yorke's book would be updated and reprinted after the war, there was more interest in "houses for moderate means" than the elaborate detached modern villas of the interwar period. Yorke's own *The New Small House* (1953) surveyed new builds since 1939—"we wondered whether there would be enough of them to make an interesting book", the author notes in the introduction. But it was clear that although the didactic appearance of 'modern' architecture had disappeared, there was improvement in other areas: "plans are generally cleaner; space is better used; thought is given to simplified housework; and more attention is given to planning for the placing of furniture… there is an intelligent use of new materials, an application of building science, houses are better insulated and heating appliances are more efficient".

Such publications were couched in terms of a modernist victory, although a true aesthetic revolution was still displaced by the necessity of reconstruction. There were still naysayers. A few years earlier, in *The Small House: Today and Tomorrow* (1947), Arnold Whittick and Johannes Schreiner had noted the popular opposition to pitched roofs—mainly because of the negative association with 'modern housing'. Perhaps it was these associations that drove post-war British architecture into its richly complex state of compromise, flushed with experimentation, steered by constraints on planning, materials and form and yet somehow rich, vital and strongly evocative of both the present and the past.

The Modernism that eventually emerged from Britain was epitomised by the idiosyncratic vision of the Festival of Britain, a world where bucolic splendour stood alongside dynamic interpretations of ultra-modern structure. Taking a very pragmatic middle path between the austere functionalism of the modernist set and more traditional visions of the national culture, 'Festival Style' was to dominate the design of architecture, furniture and products for many decades, from the textiles of Lucienne Day, the furniture of Ernest Race and design-driven companies like G-Plan and Midwinter, to the idiosyncratic planning of the new towns, with their laboured picturesque and eclectic mix of materials and

forms. The legacy of the Design Council, itself formed out of the Council of Industrial Design, the organisation that had overseen the Festival's precursor, the Britain Can Make It exhibition of 1946, was for a world of calm, rational Modernism, taking its cue from the warm embrace of Scandinavian functionalism.

In amongst all this essential change and post-war pragmatism the individual private house was necessarily overlooked. It wasn't until the 1960s that an aesthetic and theoretical consensus emerged, albeit one that was much more pluralist in its approach to 'style', not to mention location, scale and materials. Modern houses had evolved out of necessity and were no longer a provocation. By shedding the oppositional status that defined Modernism in the first half of the twentieth century, the new architecture of the era grew to be widely accepted. To live in a 'modern' house became commonplace, even desirable. Countless period houses were 'modernised', often unsympathetically, and new estates and new approaches changed the social definition of the new. In South London, the forward-thinking developer Geoffrey Townsend worked with architect Eric Lyons to create Span estates, tailored groupings of contemporary houses and apartments that were intended to 'span' the gap between high-end architecture and the banality of the everyday. Others followed. The Wates Group built great swathes of well-designed housing, while new towns like Milton Keynes and Harlow provided a well-planned canvas upon which quiet innovation could flourish.

Fashion waxes and wanes, however, and just as soon as the post-vernacular, neo-pragmatic of the 60s and 70s was accepted, it was rejected again, as Britain rode a wave of nostalgia during the 80s and early 90s. Once again, the bold forms of architect-design housing, having snuck in quietly through the catflap, found themselves thrown back out into the cold. The careful pastiche of Prince Charles and Leon Krier's Poundbury development in Dorset spawned a thousand lesser imitations. Creeping revivalism—be it Mocked-up Georgian, Revived Queen Anne Revival, Neo-Victorian or Hedgefund Tudor—physically and mentally undid the carefully constructed vision of the vital, open and empowering modern home in favour of an ersatz, domestic familiarity that hinted at both baronial splendour and bucolic isolation. The loser was contemporary design, which found itself diverted from the past to the mainstream, a trail it wouldn't pick up again for many years.

Even in the dark days of public opprobrium the modern house has always inspired enthusiasm and passion. The romantic vision of white-walled modernism was one of the driving forces behind the Thirties Society, founded in 1979 and later to become the Twentieth Century Society. Internationally there is the conservation society Docomomo, established in 1988, as well as the clusters of modernist-focused societies that exist around centres of American Modernism like Miami and Palm Springs. The social and historic values embodied by contemporary modern houses are finally being recognised, not just for their technological innovation but for their expression of a totality in design, craftsmanship and artistry that is rarely achieved. In this respect Britain, and Europe, are more advanced than the US; the Eames House in the Pacific Palisades was only designated a National Historic Landmark in 2006, whereas listing has protected many of the projects in this book. Despite their rising status, teardowns and wholesale redevelopment have to be held at bay.

Modernism had its opponents, not least because in terms of volume it has always been dwarfed by the demands of the market. The Mock Tudor of Betjeman's Metroland was dismissed cattily as Stockbroker Tudor by Osbert Lancaster, a man with an eye for architectural absurdity whatever its stripes. It was the default style of the interwar period, and while there was certainly competent Mock Tudor, as well as crisply proportioned neo-Georgian and finely detailed and beautifully executed Arts and Crafts

Opposite. Six Pillars in Dulwich, designed by Val Harding of Tecton in 1935, epitomised the Corbusian ideal translated into the British context.

mansions, the few 'Moderne' houses still stand out starkly against their identikit neighbours.

The current modern revival hasn't been substantially analysed and shows no sign of abating. What is certain is that the widespread dissemination of knowledge has buoyed contemporary architecture to a status it hasn't enjoyed for many years. Building in a contemporary style is not just widely accepted but seen as aspirational; the modern house has finally arrived. The media, the internet, the influx of new investment into Britain's transport, educational and cultural infrastructure and the relentless rise of property prices have all helped to kickstart a new interest in modern design, old and new.

The past two decades has seen a return to the boldness of the interwar years, when to commission a modern house was as much a statement about the client as the architect. The contemporary modern house is once again at the centre of culture, a nexus of architectural experimentation and new technology, materials and form-making. It has also marked a return to craftsmanship and pragmatism. New houses sit side by side with elaborate conversions and transformations of the old. Long-forgotten period pieces are once again brought back to life, restored and enhanced and published to a far wider audience than they could ever have enjoyed in their heyday. The net result is a huge rise in value and status for living in a contemporary way.

There will always be those who wish to invest and experience in these houses. In 2005, Albert Hill and Matt Gibberd established The Modern House. British estate agency has rarely been a specialist profession, except in the fields of town versus country, agricultural versus commercial and industrial. Gibberd and Hill brought a strong architectural pedigree to their small, bespoke agency, starting small in a back room and quickly landing commissions to sell some of Britain's best known contemporary houses. Both Gibberd, a senior editor at *World of Interiors*, and Hill, Design Editor at *Wallpaper** magazine, had a long association with modern design. Gibberd's architect grandfather, Sir Frederick Gibberd, designed Liverpool's Catholic Cathedral, amongst many other high-profile projects, and Hill was at *Wallpaper** while the magazine reshaped the visual landscape, highlighting long-forgotten classics and publicising the work of a new generation of architects and designers.

The agency's inaugural instruction was Six Pillars (see p 8), a Tecton-designed villa in South London. It was an auspicious start, for the signature houses of the 1930s have always proved the biggest emotional pull to modernist architecture. The agency has grown in parallel with rising public interest in contemporary design, allowing The Modern House to foreground the relationship between architecture and people, rather than design as an abstract process that happens in a vacuum. Working with the credo that "a house should lift the spirits, frame space and capture light in a life-enhancing way", Gibberd and Hill have become closely involved with many architects and estates, handling the sale of some of the most significant and iconic works of twentieth century British architecture. Their breadth of knowledge and authority makes The Modern House a creative force in contemporary architectural culture, bringing new life and fresh attention to such a vital aspect of our lives.

There is a new optimism amongst architects. The enlightened client is no longer a once-in-a-lifetime discovery but practically anyone who aspires to break out of the conventional mould. At the upper end of the market, contemporary architecture sits alongside classical revivalism

Above. Pullman Court in Streatham, South London, 1936, designed by Frederick Gibberd when he was just 23 years old. White-walled and concrete framed, the 218 apartments are spread across three blocks set amongst landscaped gardens. The latest domestic technology was used throughout.

Below. FRS Yorke's influential *The Modern House* was first published in 1934 and ran to several editions.

as the de facto means of making a mark, while a burgeoning culture of creative commissioning has seen architects work hand in hand with artists to redefine and reshape domesticity. The partnership between David Adjaye and contemporary artists like Chris Ofili, Marc Quinn, Jake Chapman, and Tim Noble and Sue Webster, has been particularly fertile, with what the studio describes as an "emphasis on light, a distinctive material and colour palette, the play between positive and negative and the ability to turn constraints into compelling narratives [as] critical themes". Architects like James Gorst, John Pardey, Carl Turner, Jonathan Tuckey Piers Smerin and David Kohn have all offered fresh interpretations of the country house, while the paucity of urban sites has provided new architectural challenges for urban living. Conversions offer another outlet for creativity, with radical and incisive interventions transforming existing houses like never before.

Taste and ideology remain uneasy bedfellows. The new architecture is a backdrop for life, a synthesis of techniques and approaches honed over decades and dovetailed into culture. The Modern House was formed to celebrate these remarkable structures and bring these individual passions to a wider audience. Contemporary architecture should be of its time, but not forgotten. These are the visions that shaped the way we want to live now and in the future.

TOWN HOUSE

The well mannered town house is one of the apexes of urbanism. To create a building that is not only harmonious in itself, but relates strongly to the surrounding structures, is a very particular architectural challenge. In many cases, the modern house broke with convention, typified by centuries of reliance on pattern books and speculative building, by standing out from its neighbours. Yet regardless of whether a modern house deferred to its context or defied it, each one represented the spirit of the age. Many were speculative ventures, often driven by the passions of young architects using themselves as a testbed for new ideas about materials and plan.

Opportunities are increasingly hard to come by. The challenge for architects and their clients is primarily about finding the space, not struggling with stylistic limitations or issues of aesthetics. The Modern House has sold many town houses since its inception in 2005. Some have displayed all the hallmarks of High Modernism's often intractable approach to context, whilst others have chosen to slip seamlessly and unnoticed into the urban fabric. Others have been steered down the path of pragmatism and raw economics, eking out the best solution on pockets of land once deemed unviable.

The need for density, sensitivity and skill shapes these houses far more than their rural counterparts, for they are bound into the fabric of history, often abutting far older structures. But despite the apparent contrast between verdant North London and quasi-industrial East London, for example, the very best architecture of the age is designed to exploit and accentuate the most desirable qualities. Greenery and vegetation become integral elements of the Gollins Melvin Ward house in Kensington and the Eldridge Smerin house in Highgate Cemetery, despite the very different contexts around each one. The historic context—be it a Hampstead terrace or Wimbledon suburb—offers the architect innumerable ways of responding, while the true tabula rasa is almost non-existent, but can still be found in backlots and brownfield sites. The Span programme created its own environments from scratch, treating landscaping and common gardens as a vital part of the design. Today's architect-led developers have far less freedom, and projects like the Herringbone House aim to maximise every precious square foot of a site.

In many respects, the modern town house is a dying breed, with conversion, restoration and hugely expensive new build the only available ways of making a mark on the cityscape. But architectural innovation never goes away. The projects shown here all highlight the response to a particular set of circumstances with a shared end goal: to improve the quality of life. Whatever the stylistic and material approach, modern living has much to offer in an urban context.

SLIP HOUSE

London SW2
Architects: *Carl Turner Architects*
2012

It has become increasingly rare to find architects building for themselves in London. The modern capital is an inhospitable environment for small-scale architectural innovation, unless economic innovation is also on the cards. Slip House occupies a South London plot between Brixton and Clapham, a small oasis of contemporary buildings growing up on a former row of garages. These unpromising brownfield sites—too small for big developers—are the last fragments of available urban space.

Carl Turner designed the Slip House as his own home and studio. Constructed from translucent glass, steel and concrete, the house takes the form of a stacked arrangement of rooms—"a simple, sculptural form of three cantilevered (or slipped) boxes". Turner built much of the project himself in collaboration with his brother, fulfilling his ambitions for "an outstanding low energy prototype house that was also serene, timeless and monastic". Since its completion, the house has won a number of awards for its design and environmental performance, including the Manser Medal.

Previous page. The translucent facade is faced with vertical glass channels, which not only allow evening light to filter through the upper storeys, but which cloak the thick, insulation-laden walls.

1 When first constructed, Slip House stood alone in the centre of its plot, accentuating the canted arrangement of the stacked floors and the stark simplicity and translucency of the vertical glass fins that clad the upper floors. Since it was finished, a new project by Turner, the Ribbon House, has been built alongside it.

2 The house has recessed windows and industrial detailing using galvanised metal and concrete.

3 Floor, ceiling and staircase are formed from polished concrete, paired with white walls and sliding doors built from whitened birch ply. The overall effect is of a house that relishes the different components of its construction, a frame into which a life has been inserted. Stair and panels were precast, delivered to site and slotted into the frame.

4 The minimal kitchen is designed to appear as monumental free-standing wooden elements in the pared-back space.

5 The main living space, with its minimal kitchen, sits above two bedrooms and beneath a roof terrace.

JAMES MELVIN HOUSE

London W8
Architects: *Gollins Melvin Ward (GMW)*
1969

This large detached house exploits its corner site and the surrounding vegetation to create an isolated, lush escape from Central London. James Melvin of Gollins Melvin Ward (GMW) designed it for his own family (although his own children had by this point grown up). GMW, which is still running, is one of the UK's leading commercial and educational practices.

The house was extensively refurbished in the 1990s by the Anglo-German firm Sauerbruch Hutton. Materials, fixtures and fittings were overhauled, and the firm's trademark bold colours were deployed on the joinery. On the ground floor, a swimming pool runs the width of the house, with Barragán-esque colours offsetting the external tropical planting. The floor-to-ceiling glazing in the first floor reception room brings the outside firmly in. New cabinetry and storage is finished in bold colours reminiscent of Sauerbruch Hutton's large-scale commercial work. The kitchen continues the polychromatic theme, juxtaposing colour with the warm tones of the new oak flooring.

In 2013, the director Joanna Hogg used the house as an integral element of her acclaimed film *Exhibition*, starring singer Viv Albertine, the artist Liam Gillick and Tom Hiddleston. It forms the domestic backdrop to a taut, complex domesticity. The director describes the house as "the perfect arena for my chamber play of encounter and emotion".

Previous pages. The rear facade overlooks the densely planted garden, and the main reception room at first floor level has two glazed facades to the south and west.

1–2 The house occupies a generous corner site, hunkering down with its dark, industrial vernacular and large windows. The entrance sequence terminates in a carport and a discrete, almost non-descript front door.

3 A still from Joanna Hogg's film *Exhibition*.

1   2

3

THE MODERN HOUSE

4

6

5

4   A modernist spiral staircase unites the floors (in conjunction with an integral passenger lift), top-lit by a prominent round roof light.

5   The ground floor swimming pool, with its Luis Barragan-style colours, is joined by a sauna and wet room. The pool room opens directly onto the garden.

6   The house is a deliberate riposte to the exuberant brickwork of the adjacent Kensington villas.

THE FRAMEHOUSE

London E9
Architect: *Marcus Lee*
2005

This complex wooden-framed house combines tight planning with structural innovation, creating a residential oasis in a North London backlot. The house was designed for his own family by Marcus Lee, a former Associate Director at the Richard Rogers Partnership, and includes a large workspace as well as five bedrooms and an open-plan living area.

The three-storey structure uses Siberian larch, red cedar and Douglas fir, with exposed framing throughout and external wooden cladding. The kitchen comprises of a double-height space adjacent to the main floorplan, expressed externally with 45 degree pitched roof, which runs through to the top floor of bedrooms. Internal planning pivots around a compact winding staircase and long corridors that run through the structure, using the grid of the wooden frame to articulate and frame views out to the garden. The house won an RIBA Award in 2009.

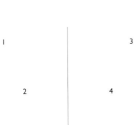

1   The wooden framed house has a high sustainability rating, with rainwater harvested off the pitched roofs. The cladding weathers naturally over time.

2   The layout of the house is independent of the structure, allowing the plan to be reconfigured as desired. The upper floor bedrooms were originally a single room, while the workspace component of the open-plan ground floor has been altered over time.

3   The kitchen is a glazed extension that opens out into the gardens, with a balcony walkway above the void to provide access to the sleeping accommodation.

4   The house is planned along traditional Japanese lines, with a long row of storage and concealed services forming a spine wall off which the other rooms are arranged. The wood is left exposed throughout.

SPAN HOUSING

Nationwide
Architect: *Eric Lyons*
1956–1984

There were around 2,100 Span homes built between the late 1950s and the mid-80s. The work of the architect Eric Lyons, working in collaboration with the developers Leslie Bilsby and Geoffrey Townsend, who also trained as an architect, Span was named after the desire to 'span the gap' between the one-off architectural commission and the mass market, developer-driven housing market. Taking inspiration from one-off architect-designed houses, each Span development was a picturesque assembly of modestly designed but well-sited properties, preserving the best qualities of each site.

In Blackheath, the Span development adjoins the Cator Estate, a collection of eighteenth and nineteenth century terraces and villas. Over time, Lyons and Townsend successfully evolved a language of small-scale domestic modernism, with Lyons developing a number of different house and apartment archetypes, including the large T15 house which is the most prominent house on the Blackheath site. Span developments placed great emphasis on space and light, and the relationship between house and landscape, both private and in shared ownership. As well as individual houses, the Blackheath development included the Hallgate apartments, a richly detailed building that paired the modernist ethos with a gentle, poetic take on the vernacular. Lyons, who began his career with Walter Gropius and Maxwell Fry, built extensively for Span and for others, as well as serving as a president of the RIBA.

TOWN HOUSE

	1		
2	3	5	6
		4	

Previous pages. A period view of the Span development in New Ash Green, and a contemporary view of Byron Court in Richmond.

1 Span housing is characterised by generous window sizes, minimal detailing and the high quality of construction. The houses and apartments are adaptable and functional for everyday life.
2 Contemporary kitchens, open-planning and a genuine sense of space shaped the Span ethos.
3 Span interiors formed a natural backdrop for the contemporary furniture of the 50s and 60s.
4 Sculpture and landscaping at Hallgate; Span developments ensured a close relationship between inside plan and generous communal outdoor spaces.
5 Byron Court in the Parkleys development in Richmond capitalised on a verdant, tranquil setting and simple, unadorned modernism.
6 Hallgate, a block of 26 apartments, was one of the centrepieces of the Span development in Blackheath, South London.

Zoe Chan and Merlin Eayrs studied at Cambridge University and the Architectural Association (the AA). Their practice combines their experience in offices like Atmos and dRMM, with whom Eayrs collaborated on the 2012 Venice Architecture Biennale with a commercial sensibility. The studio develops unpromising sites using a strong design-led approach to create bold, light-filled contemporary living spaces.

The Herringbone House occupies a 129 square metre triangular site in Dalston, tapering to a point as it steps back from the street. The firm's first major project, it brings a fresh interpretation of vernacular forms and materials with a contemporary courtyard-based layout, creating a series of interlocking living areas pivoting off a central staircase. The main facade faces south and is finished with brick courses in a herringbone pattern, running in opposing directions to create strong textural forms. The house terminates a traditional Victorian terrace, and the brick provides context alongside the pitched roof. The entrance courtyard is mirrored by a smaller courtyard at the rear of the site, creating views through the downstairs living area.

THE MODERN HOUSE

| 1 | 3 |
| 2 | 4 |

Previous pages. The street facade is dominated by the patterned brickwork and austere, stripped-back gable with its single, frameless window to the master bathroom.

1 The direction of the brickwork expresses the different areas of the house, mirroring the local fabric of change and alteration through the change in texture.

2 The kitchen is set at the rear of the triangular site and opens up onto the smaller of the two courtyards. Materials and surfaces are deliberately light and soft, increasing the refraction of sunlight through the space. The staircase is formed from steel, cantilevered from the walls with open treads and a single handrail. It leads up to three bedrooms.

3 The master bedroom occupies the eaves of the main section of the house, with an adjoining bathroom overlooking the road. The careful alignment of doors and windows sets up a view that runs the full length of the house.

4 The master bathroom uses wood, marble and glazed tiles to simple yet luxurious effect and emphasises the skewed shape of the site.

LASLETT HOUSE

Cambridge
Architect: *Trevor Dannatt*
1958

This house epitomises the strong bond between architect and client. It was designed by Trevor Dannatt for the Cambridge professor and historian Peter Laslett, and is preserved in remarkable original condition. Dannatt's career spans the entire British experience of Modernism. As a young architect he studied under Peter Moro, then later worked on the Royal Festival Hall and collaborated with Maxwell Fry and Jane Drew. He subsequently built around the world as a partner in Dannatt Johnson Architects. Throughout his life he has also written, curated and edited, overseeing *The Architect's Year Book* for a decade and a half, amongst many other publications and exhibitions. His affiliation with many of the leading contemporary architects and artists of the post-war era is evident in the rich combination of material, form and light.

1 The house is starkly elemental, with accommodation split across two levels. A dark green plinth of Holco blockwork is surmounted by a western red cedar clad box, containing the main reception room and four bedrooms.

2–3 The main reception room runs the width of the house, while a partially glazed stairwell demarcates the separation between living spaces and bedroom. A large white painted brick fireplace designed by Dannatt is a focal point, while extensive glazing provides views of the large gardens. The client was determined to make a statement of the 'modern' amidst what Dannatt describes as a "stuffy" post-war atmosphere in Cambridge.

HOUSE IN HIGHGATE CEMETERY

London N6
Architects: *Eldridge Smerin*
2008

Nestled among the elaborate gravestones of Highgate's Victorian cemetery, where Karl Marx is buried, this iconic new house replaced a 1970s dwelling designed by the late John Winter. The architect gave his blessing to the new design by Eldridge Smerin, which combines frameless glazing, concrete and granite to spectacular effect. The client, a photographer and property developer, made a remarkable discovery: he stumbled across the grave of his great-great-grandfather, just yards from the building.

From the street, the extent of the house is almost entirely concealed, thanks to the austere and private facade. However, this is countered by south- and west-facing walls of frameless glass overlooking the cemetery, creating a secluded house with an expansive relationship with its surroundings.

The new accommodation is arranged over four storeys of exposed concrete-framed structure, with a kitchen, dining room and study on the top floor, and a living room below spanning the width of the house. It is swathed with rich details and concealed technology, including a retractable glass roof to the kitchen, glass floors and a substantial basement media room. The house is also low energy, with a flowering planted roof and a thick internal concrete structure to offset the glazed facades.

1   The house forms a striking presence next to the weathered tombs and mausoleums of Highgate. Glass fins and balustrades on the upper floor terrace screen the views.

2   The internal finishes include the extensive use of textured timber shuttered concrete, giving the house great thermal efficiency and a high environmental rating.

TOWN HOUSE

BAILEY/HICKEY HOUSE

London W8
Architect: *Tom Kay*
1967

Built for the photographer Christopher Bailey and the opera singer Angela Hickey in 1967, this modernist house by Tom Kay occupies a corner site at the end of a nineteenth century terrace in Kensington. The most potent features are the cylindrical stair tower and blue Staffordshire brick facade, both of which make a stark punctuation and contrast to the surroundings without being overwhelming in scale or detail. The stair tower and slit windows have a baronial feel, creating a house with an insular, inward character that is accentuated by the use of blue brick in the interior.

Kay's plan maximised the available space of the compact corner site, incorporating an acoustically suitable double-height space for rehearsal and performance, and three bedrooms. The clients were forthright in their demands for a totally bespoke project, and once the external stair element was established, Kay's plan was able to incorporate a generously sized main reception room. The end result is a house that is simultaneously brutal and friendly, uncompromising in its form but also a welcoming and friendly diversion in the unified Victorian streetscape. Kay's esoteric approach extended to the interior fittings, making this house a rare and complete piece of urban eccentricity.

THE MODERN HOUSE

1   The double-height living room emphasises the use of birch-ply partitions and bespoke furniture to contrast with the dark blue tint of the brick. Floors are a combination of pavers and quarry tiles, offset with bespoke fittings and concrete stairs and details.

2   By placing the stair tower outside the building line, Kay made best use of the internal space. Bailey and Hickey wanted privacy, so street-facing window openings are minimal. The planners initially vetoed the use of Staffordshire brick, reasoning it was not in keeping with the area, but they were swayed by the simplicity and robustness of the forms.

3   The staircase terminates at a roof terrace (complemented by a dumb waiter system from the kitchen) and there is also a balcony off the main reception and a sunken garden to the rear. A roof light at the top of the brick drum illuminates the stair. Pragmatic details include the use of a drainpipe as a balustrade, and robust fixtures such as precast concrete light fittings that are directed either up or down against the brick walls.

DOCTOR ROGERS' HOUSE

London SW19
Architects: *Richard and Su Rogers*
1969

This modest single-storey house in Wimbledon was an important landmark in post-war British architecture. Built in the late 1960s, it spliced the aesthetic of Californian Modernism with the loose, ad hoc flexibility created through the use of high-tech industrial systems, all filtered through a bold Pop sensibility. Grade II* listed, the house was undeniably experimental, combining pre-fabricated elements, an unconcealed steel frame (engineered by Anthony Hunt) and integral furniture.

Richard and Su Rogers built the house for Richard's parents, Nino and Dada, immediately following the break up of Team 4, the practice they had formed with Norman Foster and Wendy Cheesman. It was extensively published when first completed, for it marked a distinct departure from British pragmatism. The high-tech movement

in architecture, which cemented Britain's status as a cradle of design excellence, can trace its origins to this house, and other Team 4 projects like the Reliance Controls Factory and the 'Zip Up' house concept.

It is a bold and playful building, with a flexible interior and parts taken directly from industrial applications, from windows to wall panels. The bright yellow frame and strong interior colours were a deliberate counterpoint to drab British domesticity, reflecting Rogers' own childhood in Italy, the pottery created by his mother and their collection of contemporary furniture by the Eames and Ernesto Rogers. The house remained in the family for many years, and was occupied latterly by Richard's son Ab Rogers. Plans are afoot for it to be refurbished by Philip Gumuchdjian, before being donated to Harvard's architecture school as a study centre.

Previous pages. An archive image of
the house dating from its completion
in 1969, and a photograph showing the
rear elevation today. Rogers has spoken
of the house forming a direct line to
the structural audacity and open-plan
freedom of the Pompidou Centre, which
soon became a focal point of his office.

The house forms an ever-changing
backdrop to dynamic, creative family
life, referencing eclectic modernist
treasure troves like the Eames House in
California, the bold colours of Pop art
and design and the utopian appeal of
repurposed industrial technology.

1   Industrial materials were repurposed to keep costs down and speed up the building time. Neoprene, then a relatively new material, was used to form seals and waterproofing.

2   The kitchen unit was open to the main living space, while the steel frame is prominently placed within the building envelope.

3   The steel frame allows for two fully glazed facades overlooking the garden. Over the years, the layout and function of many of the rooms has shifted, all accommodated by the flexibility of the original plan.

4   Built-in storage is paired with freestanding pieces and surviving furniture from an extensive collection assembled by Dada and Nino. The living space is subdivided by floor to ceiling sliding partitions, giving the entire house the benefit of the light from the bedrooms as well.

FOG HOUSE

London Ec1
Architects: *Adjaye Associates*
2004

The Fog House is the transformation of a former factory in Clerkenwell into a contemporary dwelling, overlooking St James' Church. It originally consisted of a long, narrow three-storey brick structure adjoining the churchyard, and was the studio of the artist Marc Quinn. David Adjaye added a new rooftop pavilion to extend the living accommodation upwards, as well as a glazed cantilever. He called it the "Fog House" on account of the sandblasted glass wall on the upper floor that creates a diffuse light.

The project was commissioned by the television presenter and broadcaster Janet Street-Porter. It was designed to provide total privacy, with a discreet entrance revealing a double-height space above a basement reception room. The three upper storeys are all open-plan and include a generously sized study, bedroom and living room respectively. Adjaye's characteristic use of bold colour and large sheets of glazing have resulted in a strong and prominent local landmark. The rooms provide a perfect frame for the eighteenth century church, with the qualities of the treated glass providing different effects depending on the height of the viewpoint.

THE MODERN HOUSE

1		3
		4
	2	5

1　The new rear facade overlooks the churchyard of St James. Adjaye added extensive glazing to the wall and roof, extending the accommodation and incorporating new roof terraces at first floor and roof level.

2　The original warehouse forms part of the narrow and ancient streetscape of Clerkenwell. Before the current conversion the property served as the studio of the artist Marc Quinn.

3　The kitchen is located on the top floor; the translucent glazing gives the house its name and provides privacy while preserving the sense of light and openness.

4　The house is arranged as a series of open-plan spaces. The main bedroom on the second floor has a free-standing bath and generous dressing room, with a free-standing storage box maximising and retaining the generous floorplan of the original building.

5　The bold use of colour is characteristic of both Adjaye's architecture and Street-Porter's personal style. The new glazed extension on the roof also allows for a private terrace that provides spectacular views of St James church.

SOUTH HILL PARK

London NW3
Architects: *Howell & Amis*
1956

The Second World War provided architects with many opportunities, large and small. This contemporary terrace of six houses in Hampstead owes its origins to a V2 bomb, which destroyed a row of grand Victorian villas, designed with their principal rooms to overlook the Heath to the south. The new buildings were designed by Bill Howell and Stanley Amis, who went on to form the firm Howell Killick Patridge & Amis in 1959. Howell discovered the site in the early 50s, and the houses were designed for his own family, for Amis, and for four other friends and close clients.

The end result is a project of remarkable coherence. Each house was custom built to the needs of its original owner, using a common system of proportion derived from Le Corbusier's Modulor. Howell and his future partners had all worked for the London County Council (LCC) on the expansive Roehampton Estate in South London. The tight proportions—each house is just 12 feet wide—were cloaked by careful planning and a deliberate avoidance of visual clutter. The occupants subsequently acquired the land between the gardens and the Heath to create communal gardens that bolster the feeling of a private community in the heart of London. The terrace featured prominently in the 1974 film *The Black Windmill* starring Michael Caine, epitomising the era's penchant for sleek modernism despite being nearly two decades old.

1

2   3

Previous pages. Seen from the Heath, South Hill Park forms part of an eclectic run of rebuilt and reconstructed infill properties in a traditionally Victorian part of London.

1   The view south across the Heath includes a parcel of land owned in trust by the six South Hill Park properties, communal gardens that were acquired later in the project's life. Each house originally contained a store and a separate one-bedroom flat at ground floor level, with a spiral staircase providing direct access to the garden.

2 The living room has a fully glazed double-height area, with a mezzanine level above. Careful detailing was used to exploit the maximum width of each narrow plot; wardrobes and cupboards were incorporated into the front elevation, there were no load-bearing internal walls and items like radiators were concealed or relocated so as not to intrude into the living spaces.

3 A study area on the mezzanine above the living room. An elegant staircase with timber treads is located in the middle of the plan, its transparency allowing light to penetrate through the space.

SHOREDITCH PROTOTYPE HOUSE

London E2
Architects: *Cox/Bulleid*
2008

The live/work space was once an archetype of urban living, from the traditional house above the shop to the rooftop workshops of the Huguenot community in Spitalfields. This four-storey house brings studio space and residential accommodation to Shoreditch, neatly anticipating the area's radical and rapid gentrification. It was designed by Tessa Cox and Oliver Bulleid on the site of a small commercial yard.

According to the architects, the project represents "a prototype low energy house for dense urban sites, and seeks to green the city through the use of vertical planting as screen, filter, sunshade and oxygenator to create a new 'garden city' in an urban context". Bolted-on steel decks provide balconies and privacy screens, while planting grown over the mesh gives shade in summer and allows direct solar heating in winter. The entrance courtyard is also heavily planted with fragrant jasmine, to create a strong juxtaposition with the towers and railway bridge that frame the view.

1   2

I   3

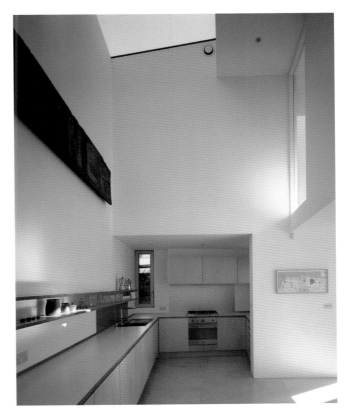

1 The green facade is created through integral planters that form part of the balconies on every floor. The ground floor studio space opens onto the front courtyard and is fringed with vegetation. Sun-shading and stack effect cooling keep the house cool in summer while exploiting the low winter sun cuts heating costs.

2 The kitchen and living area occupy the whole of the first floor level, with a top-lit double-height space located at the rear of the plan. White walls and wooden floors create a functional, contemporary aesthetic with the emphasis on natural light and minimal distraction. The double-height space is overlooked by the landing above, sequencing the ascent up through the house. Birch was used extensively for kitchen cabinets and the large flooring panels.

3 The ground floor is given over to a studio space, which is accessed via a sliding door straight off the entrance courtyard. The structure is a steel and timber frame, with specially developed woodchip blockwork panels chosen for their thermal and acoustic properties.

WINTER HOUSE

London N6
Architect: *John Winter*
1967

John Winter was one of the most significant figures in post-war British architecture. His career took him across the Atlantic, studying at Yale and then working for Skidmore, Owings & Merrill, and Charles and Ray Eames. On his return to the UK he spent time in Ernö Goldfinger's office and taught at the Architectural Association (the AA), where his students included Jeremy Dixon, Edward Jones and Nicholas Grimshaw. Winter built extensively in London in the 60s and 70s, and this house overlooking Highgate Cemetery was the second he built for his own family.

The remarkable site is accentuated by the stark modernity of the facade, and its pre-weathered Corten steel panelling was the very first time the material had been used in the UK. The panelling is mounted on a steel frame, and the house has more in common with a sleek corporate headquarters than a traditional domestic building. The reception room is placed on the top floor for maximum light and views. The Modern House sold the property for the first time since its completion following the architect's death in 2012. It has a Grade II* listing.

THE MODERN HOUSE

TOWN HOUSE

Previous pages. The Winter House is hunkered down into its site. The three storey house is surrounded by trees. Winter lived here until his death, eventually building a modest single storey ground floor extension towards the end of his life to make the house more practical. The Corten facade was constructed using the standard steel sheet, ensuring minimal wastage. This approach set up the grid; with its three by three arrangement of windows it resembles a compact and elegantly efficient office building, rendered on an exquisite domestic scale.

1   The hearth frames the room and divides living from working. The steel structure allows for long, frameless spans, while nib walls and stark, neo-Corbusian white forms create a focal point for the sitting area. Towards the end of his career, Winter worked extensively on restoring some of the major works of the early modern era, including Tecton's Six Pillars in Dulwich and William Lescaze's High Cross House in Devon.

2   The kitchen and dining rooms occupy two thirds of the ground floor. Entirely original at the time of its sale, the house featured an innovative underfloor heating system beneath the quarry tiles with their mixed patina that references the facade. The built-in kitchen was the height of modernity in 1967, with substantial storage and warm, earthy textures.

3   The top floor reception overlooks Highgate Cemetery and contained Winter's extensive library and eclectic taste in furniture—he owned a sizeable collection of original Eames pieces. These pieces served as a foil to the regulated simplicity of the structure.

1

2   3

CONVERSION

For many of the original modernist architects, the ideological approach of the new architecture was one of tabula rasa; a new movement that swept away the forms, plans, attitudes, structures and aesthetics of a bygone era in favour of a more egalitarian world. Modernism's power was in its cleansing spirt, best evidenced by the white walls, pared-back detailing and relentless emphasis on novelty, innovation and purity of form.

In stark comparison, Britain was unaccustomed to wiping slates clean. History was accumulated over centuries, attitudes were entrenched and the vernacular forms of domestic architecture were hierarchical and unassailable. The suburban villa, for example, was a direct—and self-consciously inferior—descendant of the grand country house. When the new architecture stood up and stood alone it attracted as much opprobrium as praise, but the conversion was a far more complex beast, able to slip under the radar of reactionaries and planning authorities alike.

As the century progressed, conversions have evolved from provocations to stark necessities. Few contemporary architecture practices can survive their first few years without a conversion or two or ten on the books. Happily Victorian, Edwardian and even Georgian properties lend themselves to updating, even from a radical perspective, and planners and heritage bodies have become increasingly sympathetic towards new ways of keeping old buildings up to date and in use.

The following projects are primarily a demonstration of the versatility of contemporary architecture. The deluge of unwanted commercial and industrial properties that came to market in the 80s and 90s provided yet another outlet for radical reworking. Places of worship, former factories, fortifications and agricultural buildings have all provided architects and their clients with a nearly fresh canvas upon which to explore new forms and new ways of living.

The most important component of the successful conversion is of course the intersection between old and new, preserving a sense of the utility of the past with the demands of the present. Where historic fabric is involved, such as in the Suffolk Martello Tower, the negotiation is both bureaucratic and technical, as contemporary materials and techniques offer a way of intersecting with the old causing minimal damage. Similarly, the space and light offered by industrial structures cries out to be preserved in all its majesty, allowing for bold insertions of new accommodation.

A conversion is inevitably a compromise, but as the following examples show, these compromises can be the genesis of new forms of architectural creativity.

MARTELLO TOWER Y

Suffolk
Architects: *Piercy & Company*
2009

The Martello Towers were part of a countrywide system of fortifications built during the nineteenth century. Inspired by a sixteenth century round fortress at Mortella Point in Corsica, over 100 towers were built in the UK alone, to provide a string of garrisons and guns to defend against invasion. This particular tower lies in an Area of Outstanding Natural Beauty (AONB) in Suffolk. Completed in 1808, it is listed as a scheduled monument by English Heritage.

The conversion is radical but sympathetic. Developed by the architect Stuart Piercy of Piercy & Company in collaboration with Duncan Jackson of Billings Jackson Design, it brings a deft lightness of touch to the monumental brick structure, using high-tech elements like a steel access staircase and a sculptural new roof. Taking advantage of the massive walls to house bedrooms and bathrooms, the top of the tower has been given over to an open-plan living space with panoramic views across the surrounding countryside. The conversion won an RIBA Award in 2010 and was shortlisted for the Manser Medal.

THE MODERN HOUSE

Previous pages. The tower rises up from the stark landscape, with distant sea views. The upper floor is set beneath a new roof, flooding it with light; additional circular roof lights make changing patterns of daylight across the stone floor during the day.

1   A new steel staircase leads up to the first floor entrance hall. The circular tower required an entirely bespoke approach to furniture and fittings, from the sofas in the upper floor living area to the new kitchen.

2   The main living area is located on the top floor, beneath the new roof. Raised up on slender steel pillars, the room features 360 degree glazing and a terrace, with far-reaching views to the sea beyond. The glass is frameless, the door profiles slender, and the whole ensemble is designed to have a minimal impact on the views from and of the tower.

3   The spectacular brick vault formed by the original fort structure creates a double-height space in the centre of the three metre thick original masonry (designed to protect against cannon fire), lit by small, deep windows cut into the structure. On the lower level, a camera obscura has been installed to provide a spectral view of the seaside landscape outside.

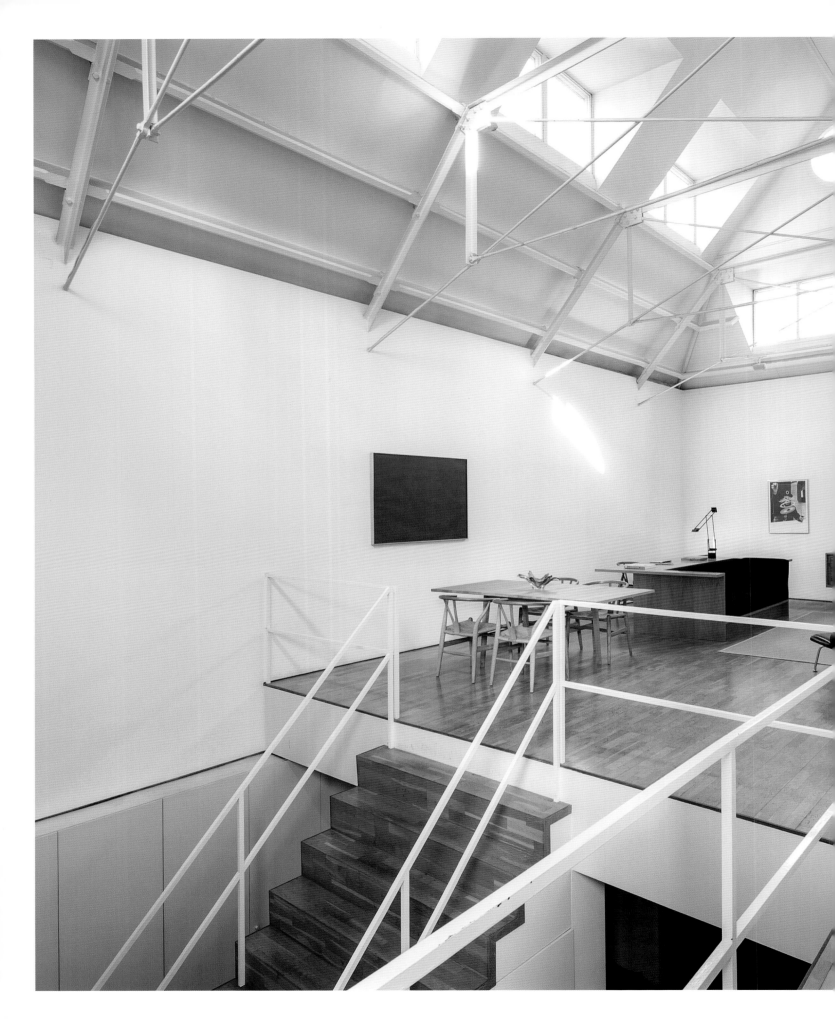

MICHAEL CRAIG-MARTIN STUDIO

London NW5
Architect: *John Pawson*
1986

Michael Craig-Martin is one of the best known artists and educators in Britain today. His former studio and home in NW5 was one of the first domestic projects of the acclaimed contemporary architect John Pawson. The original building is believed to have been a brewery for the adjacent pub. A classic piece of small-scale industrial architecture, the main space is primarily lit by a lantern of clerestory windows, leaving the exceptionally high walls on three sides completely unbroken, perfect for an artist's studio. Pawson inverted the traditional mezzanine arrangement by placing the accommodation on the lower ground floor, including a kitchen area at the foot of the precipitous staircase, a double bedroom, a dressing area and an open shower. This arrangement freed up the main floor to be as expansive and flexible as possible. Craig-Martin says: "It was originally intended to be a studio in which I would live, rather than a residence in which I would have a studio."

At the time of this project, Pawson was director of a partnership which included Claudio Silvestrin, and the Craig-Martin studio was subsequently never published. Pawson's work in the 80s and 90s came to epitomise Minimalism, as suitable for high-end stores as it was for serene warehouse apartments and private houses. Chiefly preoccupied with architectural basics—light, space, materials—he sought to minimise all visual distractions, primarily through the use of white walls without skirtings, mouldings or other detailed elements. The simple square-section balustrades and the intersection between the stair and the mezzanine illustrate Pawson's meticulous attention to detail.

1			
	3	4	
2			

Previous pages. The mezzanine living area doubles as gallery and workspace. Hand-built furniture featuring thick but highly refined oak is another Pawson hallmark (this studio featured a combined sofa and desk).

1 The studio is accessed via a small external courtyard.
2 A characteristically vivid work on canvas by Michael Craig-Martin hangs in the studio. The use of a pared-back aesthetic, including slender square-section balustrades, shadow gaps and white walls, emphasises the complexity of the original brewery ceiling.
3 Craig-Martin furnished the apartment sparsely, taking time to source original, high-quality pieces that would match the flooring and walls.
4 The staircase is a steep and complex sculptural form, uniting the levels with a minimum number of steps. The kitchen is improbably but cleverly placed on the half level, with further steps down to the bedroom and dressing room.

SHADOW HOUSE

Wiltshire
Architects: *Jonathan Tuckey Design*
2007

This chapel became surplus to requirements at the turn of the century. The Grade II* listed building dates back to 1867 and was carefully constructed in Bath stone, a scaled-down gem of a classical temple. A new addition was completed by Jonathan Tuckey Design, using blackened timber to expand the main living space to four bedrooms over 3,000 square feet and deliberately setting out to complement, not compete with, the original building. The dark, ribbed facade recalls the form and materials of tabernacle churches in the West Country, with the new component separated from the original building by a glazed link.

The new structure mimics the roof slope of the stone chapel yet it is entirely concealed from the street, as if it were the negative shadow cast. The main congregation space has become a double-height living space, with a kitchen, sitting area and dining room, while the bedrooms and bathrooms are located in the new structure. Wherever possible, original elements like floors, pews and the gallery are retained, and the limited materials palette of concrete, white painted plaster and Douglas fir fittings ensure the new element never encroaches on the honest simplicity of the chapel.

1

3   4

5

2

1   The new addition is constructed with the
    same scale, detail and proportions as the
    original chapel.
2   At ground level, the rear addition extends out
    into the garden, with contemporary detailing
    like the frameless glass corner offering a stark
    contrast with the traditional stone wall and
    classically detailed windows of the original
    chapel. A glazed link separates each element
    of the house.
3   The simple front facade conceals Tuckey's
    new extension.

4   Surviving features in the original chapel
    have been preserved, most notably the wood
    panelled gallery and flooring.
5   The rear facade takes aesthetic cues from
    the ad hoc, functional appearance of
    agricultural buildings and kit-built 'tin'
    tabernacle churches, many of which were
    erected across the UK from the middle
    of the nineteenth century.

THE RESERVOIR

Kent
Architects: *Brinkworth*
2009

A reservoir doesn't suggest a distinguished architectural approach. Instead, it implies industrial functionalism, generous scale and an almost total absence of domesticity. This substantial family house in Kent was converted from a 1930s reservoir and industrial structure for the artist Dinos Chapman and knitwear designer Tiphaine de Lussy. Brinkworth retained a substantial amount of the original structure, building a new glass pavilion on the roof to overlook the North Downs, and creating 7,500 square feet of living space.

The new house preserves the tough, concrete aesthetic of the original structure, with additional elements glazed and clad in wood to form a richly austere composition in the landscape. The main floor is divided into two areas, public and private. The principal reception room spans the entire front facade, with a retractable wall of glass doors allowing the space to be opened up to the terrace, shielded by a deep overhanging roof. The private zone consists of five bedrooms, arranged along the south elevation and united by a 25 metre swimming pool that runs outside the terrace. Garaging, studio spaces and utility areas are joined by the upper floor pavilion to create a private house that works on an industrial scale.

Previous pages. The facade shows the relationship between old and new, and the extent of the conversion.

1 A new external staircase leads down from the upper terrace, adjoining an external pool. Concrete is paired with industrial metal finishes.
2 The 25 metre pool runs the length of the south facade, shielded from view by a concrete retaining wall.

3 The lap pool adjoins the bedrooms, surrounded by tall concrete flank walls that are concealed behind an earth bank on the other side.
4 The master bedroom contains an integral bathroom. The pool is seen beyond the glazing, with steps that lead up to the roof terrace.

5 Fixtures and fittings were designed
   to fit in with the existing industrial
   setting. Concrete, wood, glass and steel
   are used with rigour and simplicity.
6 The new glass rooftop pavilion
   maximises views across the
   Kent countryside.
7 Dark brick and exposed concrete
   ceilings and polished floors are used
   throughout the main living space,
   which has a sliding glass facade that
   opens up on to the terrace beyond.

THE WORKSHOP

London NW1
Architect: *Henning Stummel*
2012

Designed and built by Henning Stummel as his own family home and architecture practice, The Workshop was ultimately sold to a prominent artist to serve as a studio. The former furniture workshop occupies a backlot behind a Victorian terrace, accessed only through warehouse doors with no indication as to what lies within. The main volume of the former workshop is preserved in its entirety, with steps that lead down to a 14 metre by 10 metre double-height living space, lit by electrically operated skylights in the steel and glass roof.

The new living accommodation forms a series of plywood boxes stacked at the far end of the space, creating an irregular internal facade. In the original scheme, the living space was further bisected by a freestanding storage unit that formed shelving for the architecture office on one side and kitchen cabinets on the other. The kitchen incorporated a dining area, and there is also a modest external courtyard accessed from this floor.

Three bedrooms are contained within two levels of the stacked boxes, one of which has its own study accessed from a small mezzanine. The original industrial building attracted the architects, despite the new design requiring the complete reconstruction of the shell. The infill nature of the site was preserved, with the drama of the entry progression accentuated by the modest entrance and the deliberate juxtaposition of the ply-faced bed boxes with the slender supports of the roof, the dark vertical steels and the polished concrete floor.

1	3
2	4

1 The project preserves the enormous internal volume of the warehouse, with the minimal steel structure preserved and contrasted with new wood interventions.

2 From the rear of the site, the industrial quality of the original building can be clearly seen.

3 The new kitchen forms one of the subdivisions of the open-plan living space, with a large free-standing island and a substantial combined table and bench used to mark out the space.

4 The kitchen storage unit also acts as a divider, aligned with the kitchen table and work area to create an installation-like landscape within the main living area. Simple wood and metal framing is juxtaposed against the original structure.

AN ART COLLECTOR'S WAREHOUSE

London N1
Architects: *6a Architects*
2012

Exploiting the linear structure of a former pianola factory, this remarkably autobiographical conversion pivots around a 26 metre living space on the first floor. Although it is one long open room, the architects have exploited the natural bays created by the roof structure to form loose areas for cooking, eating, sitting and sleeping. Their masterstroke is a series of archive cabinets set on floor runners, which can be repositioned to create different spatial arrangements. These have a multitude of functions. In the dining area, for example, they act as vitrines for museum quality ceramics, while in the bedroom they contain clothes, shoes and bags.

Every aspect of the house has been tailored for the particular needs of the client, who was heavily involved in the design process. It calls upon 6a's experience with artistic projects (the South London Gallery, Raven Row and the fashion gallery at the Victoria and Albert Museum) and bespoke commercial spaces, including Paul Smith's Mayfair store. Conservation and security technology is paired with low energy systems and solar panels, and interior elements include original bronze door furniture by 6a, tiles by Paula Rego and fossilised stone salvaged from Frederick Gibberd's terminal at Heathrow Airport.

Previous pages. The main living space is expansive, with modern insertions—ceiling, structure, lighting and IT—incorporated into the original industrial workplace.

1   The entrance hall doubles as a sitting room, with a library of books and a utility area beyond. The fossilised limestone on the floor was salvaged from Heathrow Terminal Two.
2   Original elements such as the concrete staircase have been paired with meticulously detailed new additions like these bronze and marble balustrades, designed by 6a.

3   A view along the main living space. The bays in the original roof structure create loose subdivisions, and museum archive cabinets set on floor runners can be rolled across the space for further flexibility.

4   The master bedroom is treated as a separate zone at one end of the long living room, lit by high-level windows with specially designed shelves to display art.

5   Industrial features of the original pianola factory, such as the hoist and loading bay at first floor level, are preserved and dictate the character of the conversion.

6–7   The bath is placed within the bedroom, and there is a separate top-lit shower clad in the same Heathrow stone as found in the entrance hall, with a hole blasted in the ceiling in homage to the Brazilian architect Lina Bo Bardi.

COUNTRY HOUSE

Even before the first Modern Movement buildings had appeared on British shores, it was clear that the apotheosis of the new style was best demonstrated by the stand alone house. Despite the pioneering, progressive zeal of the modernist project, the most all-encompassing examples of new architecture in Europe were private villas, commissioned by forward-thinking clients who shared the exhilarating passion for new materials, new forms and a radical break with the past, all in the name of a healthier and more vital way of living.

To a certain extent, this was also the case in the UK. Like-minded aesthetes were brave enough to bestow commissions on the newcomers, inspiring home-grown firms to explore the potential of new materials and forms in a domestic context. The great British country house had effectively died before contemporary architecture even arrived here. Many of the earliest modern villas still had accommodation for staff and a more traditional public/private divide, but they were few and far between. The country house was no longer a symbol of class and status, but a demonstration of vitality and taste. Light, space and boldness of form were eagerly adopted by the most forward-thinking, from Bernard Ashmole's commission to Amyas Connell, to Marcel Breuer in Chelsea and Sussex and the work of idiosyncratic but ideologically driven architects like Christopher Nicholson.

Connell went on to form Connell, Ward and Lucas, one of the great interwar firms, while others left the UK for greater fame—and more commissions—in America and beyond. The brief flowering of bright, white intensity was dulled then utterly dampened by the war, and the immediate post-war need for rebuilding quelled the architect-designed one-off house for a decade. When private building resumed in earnest, there was a new spirit of home-grown invention, a combination of structural boldness, formal inventiveness and vernacular materials, spliced with the beloved concrete and glass. The new generation of architects—from Womersley to Foggo, Manser and beyond—built up relatively modest portfolios of richly inventive houses, often inspired by others yet still individual.

The modern era has seen a slight return in the fortunes of the country house. Official stipulations for high design quality in rural applications have been seized upon by a new generation of architects and clients, eager to pick up the baton of innovation. The country house will always be the apotheosis of domestic architecture, a complete work of art set amidst a landscape, untrammelled by juxtaposition or context.

THE WALLED GARDEN

East Sussex
Architect: *Michael Manser*
2002

This remarkable house was inspired by the simplicity of Mies van der Rohe's Barcelona Pavilion, itself a forerunner of a whole generation of lightweight steel and glasshouses. The raised position offers up wonderful views of the Sussex countryside, while the red brick garden walls provide a rich contrast to the lawns, pools and vegetation. It was designed by the engineer Alan Murray, working with the celebrated architect Michael Manser. Manser's practice imported the spirit of American modernism into the UK, creating sleek steel-framed structures that were often juxtaposed with vernacular buildings and verdant, traditional landscapes.

The Walled Garden was designed to be deliberately timeless, adopting an aesthetic first explored in the 1920s but refined in the ensuing decades and enhanced with new glass technology and environmental performance, thanks to deep overhangs, automatic vents, special 'e' glass and underfloor heating. The house nestles right up against the original walls, which are repurposed as a dividing line between the open, glass-fronted reception rooms and the three bedrooms and two bathrooms. The clients shared the architect's meticulous attention to detail, overseeing the construction down to the finest detail ("Even the screw heads all face north–south", they noted in a newspaper article about the house). A reflecting pool cements the Miesian connection, transplanting a piece of modernist rigour into a quintessential English landscape.

THE MODERN HOUSE

Previous pages. Seen without its historic context, the new house is the perfect Miesian form, a crisp modern pavilion silhouetted against the landscape, reflected in water with the glass walls providing views of the trees beyond.

1   The new house sits atop a Victorian garden terrace, offering up far-reaching views and providing a stark contrast between brick and steel.
2   Inside, the living area benefits from glass walls and decades of mature planting. Manser's adeptness at using lightweight structural steel results in slender profiled columns, all perfectly aligned with the floor grid.
3   A modernist colonnade between the edge of the house and walls provides solar shading and a covered walkway.
4   Looking back at the original garden wall, which acts as a boundary between the more public part of the new house and the private bedroom area. The master bedroom, shown here, occupies the most private aspect of the glazed structure.

FARNLEY HEY

West Yorkshire
Architect: *Peter Womersley*
1954

Farnley Hey represents a fine example of the eclectic mode of British Modernism. Designed in 1954 by the architect Peter Womersley (intended as a wedding present for his brother), the house occupies a prime position on the edge of the Pennines, a site it exploits with tall windows in the majestic living area. The composition is a spirited, playful assemblage of forms and materials that evokes the optimism of the age of its construction, as well as the influence of Frank Lloyd Wright and Le Corbusier. Wood cladding, York-stone floors, Formica panelling, period patterned tiles, brick, slender steel balustrades and built-in furniture (and a sound system) all combine to create a harmonious and original structure. The house was one of the first post-war buildings to be listed and remains in remarkable condition.

Farnley Hey was the start of a varied and often experimental career, throughout which Womersley concentrated on private residential design, although he also built larger educational and healthcare projects. His work explored a variety of materials, exploiting the structural and sculptural possibilities of concrete in particular. Modest in scale, powerful in form and richly crafted, it demonstrated Modernism's potential as an architecture for every application.

COUNTRY HOUSE

2

1

3

Previous pages. The house shortly after completion when occupied by its first inhabitant, Womersley's brother and his wife. At the right is a contemporary photograph of the garden facade, illustrating the architect's use of different materials to emphasise the house's various zones, including the large living space at the left.

1   The living rooms are raised up to maximise views across the moors.

2   The changes in level, material and orientation showcase an eclectic take on modernism, inspired by the idiosyncratic but spatially ingenious works of Le Corbusier and Frank Lloyd Wright.

3   The house incorporated the latest domestic technology, including a built-in sound system flanking the brick-faced fireplace. A terrace looks out across the moors.

THE MODERN HOUSE

RED BRIDGE HOUSE

East Sussex
Architect: *Piers Smerin*
2013

This striking contemporary house nestles in a 22 acre site in the East Sussex countryside. The project was a rare opportunity to build a completely new house in a spectacular location, and the architect Piers Smerin indulged the clients with a stripped-back palette of materials, creating a three-storey house that acts as a foil to the surrounding landscape without overpowering it. It is built using a steel frame, allowing for an asymmetric overhanging roof to provide shelter for the double-height veranda outside the living area. The lower ground floor contains a pool opening directly onto the garden. The modular steel frame is paired with concrete floors and timber cladding on the garden elevations, allowing for long column-free spaces and the potential for future conversion and alteration. The entrance facade—across the 'red bridge'—is finished in weathered steel, evoking the region's agricultural buildings.

1 The new house sits on a bluff atop a sloping site, with the land falling away from the double-height reception space and balcony at first floor level. The purity of the wood-clad facade is tempered by the asymmetric forms of both roof structure and internal balcony, adding a sense of chiselled dynamism to the house.
2 At ground floor level is a swimming pool, surrounded by sliding glass doors that can be completely opened up to the gardens. The sparse palette relies on the adept use of just a few materials: concrete form walls, ceiling and floor.

STRATTON PARK

Hampshire
Architects: *Stephen Gardiner and Christopher Knight*
1964

Stratton Park is one of the few genuinely iconoclastic modern houses in the UK. Commissioned by Sir John Baring, it replaced an 1803 mansion by George Dance the Younger, originally remodelled for Sir Francis Baring. Dance's main addition was a mighty Doric portico, which was retained in its entirety, with a new house created behind it to the designs of Stephen Gardiner and Christopher Knight. The new house is built largely of brick with a glazed, double-height conservatory. It has dramatic landscape views, framed by the four substantial columns of Dance's portico.

Gardiner enjoyed a long career, primarily as a writer, biographer and teacher, and worked with Richard Sheppard in the early 1950s. His interests and expertise ranged from Le Corbusier to Jacob Epstein, and he was a strong critic of contemporary architecture, often bemoaning the loss of human scale and "warm, personal" materials in favour of rigour and austerity.

Previous pages. Looking back at the new house, with the original portico in the far distance, showing the landscape originally laid out by Humphrey Repton and subsequently added to by Gertrude Jekyll.

George Dance's mighty portico survives as a frame for Gardiner and Knight's new house. The separation of old and new creates a jarring frisson, and stands as a stark statement of the relationship between the traditional country house and the new architecture.

The Doric portico is viewed through the wonderfully rambling double-height conservatory, which is almost entirely glazed. An external pool creates additional reflections.

SEA LANE HOUSE

West Sussex
Architect: *Marcel Breuer*
1936

Marcel Breuer came to the UK from Germany for just three years after leaving his architecture post at the increasingly threatened Bauhaus. As well as working for Isokon, he designed and built this house in collaboration with FRS Yorke, which is a rare example of the cross-pollination between European Modernism and its fast-evolving British counterpart. A striking composition of concrete, brick and glass, Sea Lane House is raised above its site on oblong pilotis, with two garages, a kitchen and entrance hall at ground floor level. Upstairs, a long projecting wing contains six modest bedrooms and a large living room and dining room, adjacent to a curvaceous sun terrace with stairs down to the garden.

The raised structure provides sea views and improves natural daylighting (both Breuer and Yorke were also well aware of Le Corbusier's famous stipulation of the ideological and aesthetic value of pilotis). Deliberately intended as a riposte to 'period mannerism', the house remains an expressive and bold statement, a forerunner of the architect's later and more elaborate sculptural work in the USA. Owned for the vast majority of its life by a pioneering automotive engineer, Richard Papelian, it was sold by The Modern House to a fashion designer, who has been exploring the potential for sensitive restoration.

1   Sea Lane House has an elemental relationship with its site, raised up so as to glimpse the sea and unashamedly nautical in terms of detailing and form.
2   The sun terrace is the most virtuoso element of the design, a curved concrete element that leads from living room to garden level. Breuer was soon to leave Isokon and the UK for America, where his domestic architecture evolved into a more ad hoc and expressive style.

1

2

COUNTRY HOUSE

THE LONG BARN

Wiltshire
Architects: *Klaentschi and Klaentschi*
2001

The barn offers a 'promise of scale' unavailable to the conventional homebuilder or buyer. This new house in Wiltshire by Hans and Paula Klaentschi was designed as a home and studio for the architects, but took inspiration from working structures in the surrounding countryside, both in terms of simple, rough-edged aesthetics and the sheer physical scale of a large enclosed space beneath a pitched roof. As a result, one end of the house is dominated by a large double-height space, with walls and ceiling clad in Russian ply to emphasise the scale and agricultural inspiration for the long structure. A Swedish timber frame forms the core, allowing for easy alterations to the internal layout in the future. A row of roof lights runs down the ridgeline, creating a constantly shifting pattern of natural light, especially in the towering reception and studio rooms.

1

2   6

3   4   5   7

Previous page. The Long Barn exerts an agricultural character, nestled into its site with an unbroken roof profile and deep overhanging eaves.

1   The double-height studio and storage area exemplifies the pragmatic, rough and ready quality of low-cost materials and straightforward finishes.
2   The house's barn-like character is most immediately obvious from the access road approach.
3   The side elevations are more conventionally contemporary, with the rear of the building given over to a large glass-walled studio/storage space for the storage and display of classic cars.

4   External openings are dictated by the size and shape of standard panels of wood cladding to keep costs down.
5   The detail design is prosaic and functional.
6   Internal surfaces are clad in Russian ply, creating a bold, highly tactile and sensuous experience. The mezzanine study sits above the double-height living area.
7   Expansive windows are paired with small clerestory lighting to determine the shape and perception of the room and maximise natural light in the densely planted plot.

High & Over is a definitive work in the evolution of the modern country house. It was commissioned by Bernard Ashmole, who later became director of The British Museum. In Amyas Connell, he found an architect willing to not just imitate the crisp white walls of the new continental style, but improve on it, creating a house that transcended the gaudy stylings of Art Deco despite its rich use of materials like chrome and marble, its glass-encased spiral staircase and circular swimming pool. The building was an avant-garde shock that symbolised the start of a new architectural order, viewed admiringly by Pevsner as well as the not-always-modern-friendly *Country Life*.

The house's history is also symptomatic of the wider shifts that have affected pioneering modern structures in the UK. Subdivided and altered, with additions removed and encroaching suburbia on all sides stripping the 'country house' appellation and dulling its splendid white-walled isolation, High & Over fell out of favour, like so many houses of its ilk. Renovation and restoration were time-consuming and expensive, especially given the advanced and often experimental nature of its original reinforced concrete construction, but today the ground floor has been returned to its original plan and colour scheme.

		3
2		4

Previous pages. The mature landscape surrounding the house is very different from its original bare 12 acre hillside plot. The stark white concrete has weathered with age yet the house retains its bold, uncompromising form.

1   The shaded top floor terrace was an obvious nod to European Modernism, but was also a space for the clients' children. The nursery was at second floor level and the roof functioned as an extension of the playroom.

2   The original landscaping was devised by Connell and Ashmole, with a pool added on the main axis in 1934. Orchards, lawns, ornamental beds and outhouses, including a water tower and gardener's lodge, were all included in the scheme.

3   The circular opening in the heart of the house. High & Over is no ultra-functional machine for living; the details and materials are rich, decorative forms are in evidence and Connell was happy to accommodate the tastes and desires of his cultured clients.

4   The original design included built-in furniture, light fittings and furnishings. The ceilings are suspended, with the light boxes shown here installed between the concrete beams.

THE MODERN HOUSE

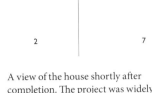

1 A view of the house shortly after completion. The project was widely acclaimed, with the procession from entrance to reception room being particularly praised.
2 The house today, sitting on a well-tended and generous private site that greatly enhances the relationship between architecture and landscape.
3 The main reception room is in the tradition of a grand salon, only with the addition of wood-clad ceilings and mustard yellow carpets.
4 Gooday combined raw concrete with painted brick and wood, expressing structure and using built-in storage as architectural elements in their own right.
5 The room opens out onto a small garden terrace, with surfaces continued out of the interior into the landscape.
6 A small mezzanine study area is accessed from a spiral staircase and fitted with custom-built storage.
7 A period photograph of the house illustrating Gooday's interior schemes and sparse, elegant furnishings.

LONG WALL

Surrey
Architect: *Leslie Gooday*
1962

This spectacular Grade II* listed house, designed in 1962 by the acclaimed architect Leslie Gooday for his own occupation, can be found on a beautiful secluded and landscaped site of approximately two acres.

The approach is through a courtyard that leads to the front door and into a terrazzo hallway whose dynamic design gives a taste of the exhilarating architecture beyond. To the left, a run of bedrooms and bathrooms reaches out into the landscape, while straight to the right is the spectacular main reception room, a virtuoso composition featuring soaring birch ceilings, a board-marked concrete wall and almost an entire wall of glass giving elevated views across the lush, landscaped gardens. It is also notable for a fireplace with recessed arches above a low-level cantilevered concrete shelf that runs the length of the living space.

Materials were carefully chosen and meticulously applied, from the board-marked concrete to the copper mansard roof and extensive built-in cupboards, fixtures and storage. The reception room has two terraces overlooking the gardens, which slope away from the house. Leslie Gooday had a long and distinguished career, starting as an assistant to Hugh Casson on the Festival of Britain and being awarded an OBE for his design work on Britain's pavilion at Expo '70 in Osaka, Japan. The house was widely acclaimed on completion, with the procession from entrance to reception room being particularly praised.

OCHRE BARN

Norfolk
Architects: *Carl Turner Architects*
2011

The sheer luxury of space is embodied in Carl Turner's pared-down approach to this contemporary barn conversion. Over 500 square metres of space is joined by a separate studio building, the Stealth Barn. The conversion of a former Victorian threshing barn, the project is composed of two wings, one of which is given over entirely to a 200 square metre reception room and kitchen/dining area, alongside which runs a five bedroom accommodation wing.

Externally, the barn's brick skin is preserved and restored, while the interior walls are rendered and painted, as are the trusses and steel of the roof structure. New openings are detailed and scaled to match the originals. Turner's firm designed and built the project itself, with bespoke interior fittings made from richly textured Oriented Strand Board (OSB), creating blocky elements that recall both hay bales and the geometric forms of artists Richard Serra and Donald Judd. Polished concrete floors and concealed storage—even in the kitchen—keep the vast space clear and uncluttered.

Previous pages. The Ochre Barn contains bedrooms in the long, low original structure, enhanced with new doorways and openings, while the live/work space is located in the taller barn behind.

1 The Stealth Barn, a self-contained studio building, sits adjacent to the main house, seemingly set down in the landscape.
2 The main living space is punctuated by new additions, storage and furniture made from OSB.
3 The new rooms exploit the high ceilings of the original barn space, with minimal partitions and subdivisions and exposed timbers and truss structure.
4 The interior of the Stealth Barn. OSB creates dense, intimate spaces, with intersecting planes forming a chunky, solid structure as if they have been carved from a solid block of the material. It also evokes the hay bales that were once stored in the barn.

LONG WALL

Suffolk
Architect: *Philip Dowson*
1963

The early 1960s were a fertile period for modern residential architecture in the UK. Long Wall was originally commissioned as a weekend house, and the client appointed Philip Dowson of Arup Associates to complete a simple, single-storey design. Dowson worked in collaboration with his colleagues Peter Foggo and Max Fordham. The house is modest in scale, opening up on three sides to the garden with the 'long wall' running through the site and into the landscape to frame and structure the interior space. Extensively restored and refurbished by Hugh Pilkington in 1995, it retains the qualities that saw it compared to buildings by Mies van der Rohe and Philip Johnson, an understated element in the landscape that draws its power from the juxtaposition of glass, wood and brick with the lawns and trees. Dowson's approach was famously low-key and site-specific, a quality he brought to many of the other projects he oversaw at Arup Associates, notably the Snape Maltings Concert Hall at Aldeburgh and his work at Oxford and Cambridge.

1 The titular 'long wall' is painted bright white, and neatly bisects the house's garden facade. Influenced in part by Frank Lloyd Wright's extension of architecture into landscape, as well as Mies' approach to the pavilion amongst nature, the house makes a quietly powerful statement.

2 The entrance approach keeps the relationship between house and garden concealed, although the ordering wall is still a key element in the composition.

1

2

EAGLE ROCK

Sussex
Architect: *Ian Ritchie*
1981

One of the pre-eminent projects of the early high-tech era, Eagle Rock was designed for a client who wanted to emphasise the avian nature of the design, inspired by the surrounding fauna. The house therefore became what Ritchie describes as a "metaphor of suspended flight", with two glazed wings rising up and away from a central spine, with a raised "crest" of steel from which the structure is suspended, and a tail element that is a "crystal greenhouse". The approach was also rooted in climatic concerns so as to minimise the need for additional heating or ventilation. Many of the interior finishes were carried out by Ritchie and his Architectural Association (the AA) students. The house combines ultralight elements with a solid core, reaching out into the surrounding gardens.

This combination of art and sculpture characterises Ritchie's work. As well as working with Norman Foster early in his career on the Willis Faber Building, Ritchie collaborated with Peter Rice of Arup and the yacht designer Martin Francis to form Rice Francis Ritchie (RFR), and also taught alongside Mike Davies at the AA. Eagle Rock was his first major architectural project, and he benefited from the cross-disciplinary approach pioneered by RFR. In 1987 he left the consultants and set up his own studio, with major works including the Reina Sofia Museum of Modern Art in Madrid and Bermondsey Station on the London Jubilee Line extension.

THE MODERN HOUSE

1   3

2   4

1   Viewed from above, the bird-like shape of the plan is immediately obvious.
2   The 'beak', or entrance section, with its raised up, crest-like roof pylons supporting the oversailing canopy above the entrance way.
3   Eagle Rock is a prototypical high-tech structure, combining industrial materials and approaches with a more typical domestic scale. The large wing-like spans were achieved with long metal trusses, all of which are expressed outside of the structure.
4   At the intersection of body and wings is a double-height space, around which the house pivots, providing vistas down each wing and along the body.

AUGUSTUS JOHN STUDIO

Hampshire
Architect: *Christopher Nicholson*
1933

Originally built as a studio for the artist Augustus John, this house sits in the grounds of Fryern Court, John's Hampshire manor house. The architect was Christopher 'Kit' Nicholson, younger brother of the artist Ben Nicholson and son of painters Sir William Nicholson and Mabel Pryde. Nicholson studied and then lectured at Cambridge, where he taught Hugh Casson, who he subsequently collaborated with. He was a lifelong aviation enthusiast, and designed the striking London Gliding Club in Dunstable. Unfortunately this passion was to be his undoing, and he died prematurely in a gliding accident in Italy in 1948.

Nicholson's design for John was utterly dedicated to purpose, featuring one large high-ceilinged studio room lit by full-height windows at either end, and a series of window niches, each furnished with a concrete bench for models to recline. The studio was raised up on sturdy pilotis to maximise the available light in the densely planted gardens, and accessed by a sculptural twist of a concrete staircase, designed in collaboration with the engineer RG Robinson. Originally, the downstairs consisted of a 'strong room', where John could lower his completed canvases for secure storage.

The forms, composition and structure all reference Nicholson's interest in Modernism and abstraction. Following John's death, the studio was converted into a dwelling in 1973, with new bedroom accommodation filling in the bulk of the ground floor and the studio preserved as a grand reception room. The Modern House subsequently sold it to a well known sculptor, in a fitting continuation of its artistic legacy.

2

1   3

Previous page. An archive photograph of the studio showing the ground floor level before infill works.

1   The studio today, with accommodation added amongst the support pilotis on the garden floor and the twisting concrete staircase leading up to the studio space terrace.

2   The studio in Augustus John's day; high ceilings, natural light and plenty of perches for models to pose before the artist.

3   The large window provides north light, with modelling niches arranged along the east facade.

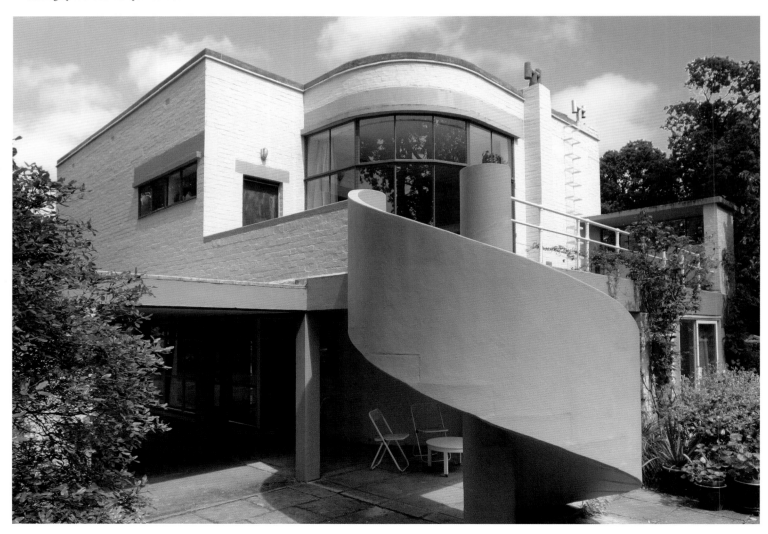

MANOR WAY

Berkshire
Architects: *Peter Foggo and David Thomas*
1962

One of the most vivid evocations of the Case Study House series ever built in the UK, Manor Way is home to a group of three dwellings by Peter Foggo and David Thomas. Constructed in the early 1960s, the single-storey houses have exposed steel frames and are raised slightly off their site. The H-shaped plans are arranged around a central service core flanked by two wings, one containing the bedrooms and the other the kitchen/dining area, with a large square living room in the centre facing the gardens with floor-to-ceiling glass throughout.

Designed in the architects' spare time (both were working at Arup), the Manor Way houses were part of a select group of contemporary structures built by Foggo and Thomas, all of which embodied their love of Miesian simplicity and the glamour and lightness of the Californian Case Study Houses. In recent times these houses have been neglected and largely ignored. Their discovery by sympathetic owners (all three via The Modern House) has resulted in extensive restoration and a return to the aesthetic values that Foggo and Thomas were almost alone in championing back in the 60s.

1   3

2   4

Previous pages. The houses in Manor Way are classically symmetrical, raised up on a shallow plinth that sets them apart in pristine isolation from the landscape.

1 The H-shaped plan provides plenty of viewing angles across and through the house between the wings. Foggo and Thomas' experience of commercial architecture is evident in the strong, unfussy detailing.

2 Glazed walls fill the reception rooms with light. The dining room adjoins the kitchen, a near 50 foot long room forming one 'wing' of the plan.

3 The entrance hall is flanked by a terrace, at the left, and a central core to the right that houses the bathrooms and utility area. The bedroom wing is straight ahead, with infill wooden panels set within the steel frame.

4 The square living room has a glazed wall and corner windows that project out into the garden.

AHM HOUSE

Hertfordshire
Architects: *Jørn Utzon and Povl Ahm*
1962

2

1

Previous pages. As well as emphasising a strong relationship between the interior and garden, the house was a showcase for Danish product design, including these original leather Arne Jacobsen Egg chairs and stools, designed in 1958.

1 The house is exquisitely detailed, with a roof supported by longitudinally placed concrete beams that also form a ribbon of clerestory windows at each end of the house.

2 Placed in a corner of the plot, the house is designed to extend into the landscape with terraces and walls that reach out to embrace the garden.

Created from an initial design by the Danish architect Jørn Utzon—who never visited the site—in collaboration with his client, the civil engineer Povl Ahm, this is a very Scandinavian house set in very English countryside. Utzon and Ahm, a former chairman of Ove Arup, worked together on the Sydney Opera House, the hugely complex project that made, undid and ultimately cemented Utzon's reputation. The Hertfordshire house was far more straightforward, a long, low pavilion of yellow London brick combined with bold structural precast longitudinal beams that project beyond the line of the windows.

Over Ahm's long career he worked with Basil Spence on Coventry Cathedral and Arne Jacobsen at St Catherine's College, Oxford. His close relationship with architects—and the struggles Arup went through to achieve Utzon's vision in Sydney—is evident in the detail and purity of his own house. The building took two years to complete, testament to the care and attention lavished on its construction, from the teak mullions and fittings to the white Swedish Höganäs floor tiles, which extended out onto the terrace to bring the outside into the living space. Together with his wife, Birgit, Ahm filled the house with furniture and objects that celebrated his Danish heritage. In 1974, the architect Ulrik Plesner added another wing to match the original structure, all of which remained concealed from its more conventional suburban neighbours.

3   The main living area has high ceilings, with changes in level throughout the plan to the bedrooms and kitchen. The internal flooring is continued out onto the terrace.

4–5 The bespoke timber kitchen is open to the dining area via a serving hatch, with honey-coloured brick and timber matched to the tile floor and cast concrete ceiling.

6   The top-lit bathroom appears like it has been carved out of brick, with every measurement and alignment precisely controlled.

APARTMENT

Some of the earliest modernist buildings were apartments, expressing not just the structural possibilities of new materials, but the liberating spaces for living they created. The apartment building was the zenith of Modernism's socially progressive ambitions, a direction ploughed extensively and exhaustively by its strongest proponents on the continent, most famously (and some would say notoriously) Le Corbusier. In the UK, as with private housing, it was often a very different story.

At the turn of the twentieth century, the apartment didn't have the same image it did in Europe. Urban apartments were rare; the grand brick-built mansion blocks of the Edwardian era were the closest parallels to their equivalents in Paris or Berlin, and most were aimed at the wealthy upper middle class.

The new architecture spurred interest in apartment building design. By 1937 FRS Yorke was on the case, writing *The Modern Flat* in collaboration with Frederick Gibberd.

Perhaps the greatest victor in the rush to building truly modern flats was Art Deco. True Modernism remained thin on the ground—save for projects like Highpoint, Pullman Court and the Isokon Building—but Deco segued seamlessly into the domestic narrative, updating stuffy brick Edwardian architecture into sleek, sensuous forms.

After the war, the groundwork laid by modernist form and structure was ruthlessly deployed, often skilfully, more often not, across towns and cities desperate for new housing to replace bomb-damaged and inferior stock. Projects of unprecedented quality and generosity of space were frequently lumped in with the less prepossessing examples. The wholesale clearance of bomb-damaged communities into shiny new tower blocks ultimately tainted the image of modern architecture as a powerful social force for good. Perhaps the ultimate British expression of Modernism's totality-or-nothing approach was the Barbican, the vast residential complex that succeeded not only because of design, but luck, longevity and the persistence of its architects.

The modern apartment is not always a purpose-built proposition. As cities and structures evolve and use changes, the plethora of industrial conversions and transformation has given architects and clients new opportunities. Building in between or above the townscape might not have figured in Modernism's pioneering early days, but architectural invention has given fresh life to every facet of contemporary apartment living.

ISOKON BUILDING

London NW3
Architect: *Wells Coates*
1934

The Isokon Building sailed into interwar London on a wave of celebrity and glamour. Developed by Jack and Molly Pritchard of the Isokon company, it was designed by Wells Coates to be a contemporary statement of communal living. Completed in 1934, it was the nexus of interwar Modernism, attracting not just the young professionals it was aimed at, but artists and writers as well as many of the designers who collaborated with Isokon itself.

Wells Coates was immersed in the intellectual world of Modernism, attending the seminal 1933 Congrès International d'Architecture Moderne (CIAM) conference and establishing the Modern Architecture Research Group. He wholly embraced contemporary materials and production methods, advocating modular construction, compact living spaces and minimal, albeit fluent and elegant design. The Isokon Building contained around 30 modest apartments as well as staff quarters and shared kitchens, which were converted into a communal club, the Isobar, in 1937. White, sleek and stark, and built mostly of reinforced concrete, the Isokon was defined by the bold staircase and communal balconies, creating a linear, almost nautical form amidst Hampstead's verdant lanes. The majority of apartments are modest in scale, and originally came with built-in furniture (much of it produced by Isokon itself).

For the public, the Isokon Building's most prominent resident was undoubtedly crime novelist Agatha Christie, who lived there during the war. It was also favoured by artists—Paul Nash had a flat there, and Barbara Hepworth and Ben Nicholson were regulars at the Isobar. Thanks to Pritchard and Coates' contacts amongst the European design scene, the building played host to many émigré designers. Most notably, Walter Gropius spent three years living in the building, and working as Controller of Design for the company. He was succeeded by Marcel Breuer. László Moholy-Nagy and James Stirling also spent time in the building, as did the Soviet spy Arnold Deutsch.

The Pritchards lived in the penthouse, despite the Isokon company itself falling victim to the wartime appropriation of its plywood quota. The apartment is now occupied by Magnus Englund, managing director of Skandium, who has been instrumental in the creation of a gallery in the building's converted garage space in recent years. The Isokon survived a period of abandonment to be extensively restored by John Allan of Avanti Architects in 2004.

THE MODERN HOUSE

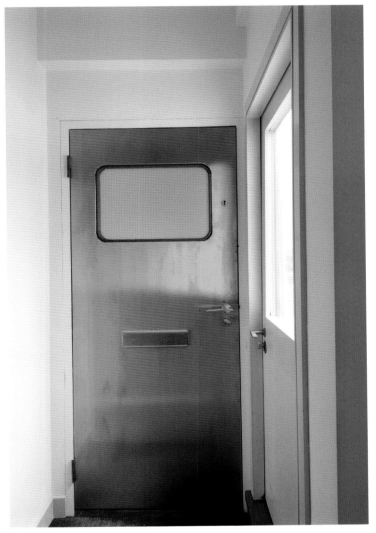

1		
	3	4
2		

Previous pages. The Isokon Building is now Grade I* listed, the highest level of official protection. It is once again a fashionable place to live, rescued from near dereliction and possible demolition back in the 1970s.

On completion in 1934, the Isokon Building was progressive in materials, form and social structure, creating a stark rejoinder to its traditional brick-built surroundings.

1 The Isokon Building's apartments—even the Pritchards' own penthouse—were modest by the standards of the day, designed for professional people without room for servants. This room illustrates many examples of Isokon furniture, including Ernest Race's Donkey 2 from 1963 and a sofa by Marcel Breuer.

2 Bedrooms and bathrooms were functional, with built-in furniture and storage.

3 A restored bathroom showcases the tight spatial planning.

4 The front door of the penthouse; Pritchard was not a strict minimalist, but the building resembled a marked attempt to reinvent the contemporary apartment.

ROOF GARDEN APARTMENT

London EC2
Architects: *Richard Rogers and Tonkin Liu*
2002

Adapting and reusing urban space isn't confined to reshaping existing buildings. Sometimes, the best solution is to go up, and create new spaces atop the existing fabric. This apartment is the radical addition of a new steel structure above a brick warehouse, shaping a generous living space that not only grows out of the original building, but adds a layer of vegetation and form to the rooftop landscape.

The design is acclaimed for the way in which the rigorous grid of the steel structure stands at odds with the brick below. The apartment makes explicit use of simple industrial materials and objects, such as the galvanised steel spiral staircase and metal mesh, which doubles as a plant screen. A double-height reception area sits above a floor of bedroom accommodation, with a roof terrace above.

Building above the existing city infrastructure offers a world of opportunity for the brave and patient. This apartment not only created a family home in otherwise 'vacant' space, but greened the city skyline in the process.

3
2
1
4

1 The new structure appears to be extruded from the existing warehouse, with new steels set above the original brick piers and a snaking canopy of planting rising up into the sky.

2 The upper floor of the new addition is given over to a double-height living area, with stunning views of London's skyline.

3 A terrace encircles the lower level, providing additional outdoor space for the bedrooms as well as the roof terrace on the summit of the apartment. The planting provides privacy and verdant views, despite the location. A spiral staircase links the terraces.

4 The lower floor contains a sunken seating area for watching films, boldly coloured and detached from the urban landscape outside.

PROVENDER MILL

Bruton, Somerset
Architects: *Mark and Lucy Merer*
2001

An early example of steel-frame construction, Provender Mill was a former grain mill, a stark but elegant structure built in the 1940s that had always seemed out of place in the historic Somerset market town. The 2001 conversion, overseen by sculptors Mark and Lucy Merer in collaboration with Mark's father, Stanley Merer, exploited the mill's dark, industrial good looks. It was designed with the town's industrial history in mind, retaining a working studio component whilst adding a new apartment at second and third floor level. The Modern House sold it to a renowned contemporary artist, who carried out further refurbishment in collaboration with the architect Paul Fineberg.

The structure maintains its original form, with the black cladding referencing local agricultural buildings and contrasting with the roofs and stone walls of the surroundings (the local historical society gave the project a conservation award in 2002). The new apartment is raised up above the roofs and has panoramic views through large frameless windows. A sculptural freestanding fireplace unit, designed by Stanley Merer, forms a centrepiece.

THE MODERN HOUSE

Previous page. The building is a prominent structure in the ancient town, rising above the stone and slate roofs.

1   The conversion integrates a substantial new apartment in the upper floors of the old mill, with new window openings and a facade in the spirit of the original building.

2   The main living space has views across the old town. Arranged around a new free-standing fireplace, it references the former industrial use of the building while also evoking the spirit of an urban loft apartment.

3   Throughout the rebuilt upper floors, new steel structure and roofing elements are given a prominent place in the living spaces.

BARBICAN ESTATE

London EC2
Architects: *Chamberlin, Powell and Bon*
1975

One of the most successful post-war housing projects, the Barbican defies easy definition. Originally intended as an entirely new, self-contained city district, it contains over 2,000 apartments, as well as public green spaces, an arts complex, library, museum and schools. The coherence of the architecture and close proximity to the City of London lent the apartments great social cachet from the outset, so the estate suffered none of the social problems typically attributed to large-scale modernist developments (especially those that used large quantities of exposed concrete structure).

As a result, the Barbican remains a hugely successful anomaly, unlikely to be replicated on such a scale again (at least in the UK). Despite replacing large swathes of bomb-damaged London, the estate's architects weren't appointed until the mid-1950s and its construction didn't begin until 1965, lasting well over a decade. The Barbican Centre itself finally opened in 1982. Despite the drawn-out process, the solidity and coherence of the architects' original plans set the buildings apart from passing fads. Externally, the Barbican's rough, jack-hammered concrete fins have endured, passing in and out of fashion and back in again, their Brutalist forms finding favour amongst a new generation.

Inside, the Barbican displays a huge variety of apartments and maisonettes, with over 100 types. Chamberlin, Powell and Bon placed great emphasis on internal planning and the quality of fixtures and fittings, especially kitchens and bathrooms, taking inspiration from yacht design to save space and using the latest appliances. Originality is still prized, and the estate's listed status and strict management policies do much to bolster the sense of a self-contained community within the city. Grander flats have double-height spaces, barrel-vaulted roofs, transformable floor plans and generous terraces, while attention to detail pervades every inch of the buildings, inside and out.

Previous pages. The Barbican is a bravura piece of placemaking, with bridges, ramps and endless staircases creating a multiplicity of routes through the concrete and brick complex.

The three towers—Cromwell, Lauderdale and Shakespeare (the last to be completed, in 1976)—were for many years the tallest residences in the city. Triangular in plan, each presents a saw-edge of concrete balconies with views to the city.

1   Built-in appliances, such as this original Creda cooker, are much sought after by design-savvy residents keen to preserve authenticity.
2   Other labour-saving devices included waste disposal units, then a rarity in the UK.
3   Despite the extensive landscaping, the complex was criticised by some for its elevated walkways and confusing signage.
4   Apartments originally contained an externally accessible storage cupboard for post, parcels and deliveries.
5   A double-height top-floor apartment, one of the more lavish and spacious typologies in the Barbican.

1

2

3

5

4

THE MODERN HOUSE

LOST HOUSE

London N1
Architects: *Adjaye Associates*
2003

The Lost House is the work of David Adjaye, commissioned by the fashion entrepreneur Philip de Mesquita and designer Roksanda Ilincic. It is bold, deliberately provocative and theatrical, with an emphasis on spaces for entertaining and display. Despite its name, the property is in fact a leasehold apartment. It was built on a delivery yard adjacent to a King's Cross warehouse, and retains a concealed, hidden facade with little indication of what lies within.

The apartment has a huge 18 metre reception room at its heart, lit by three large light wells forming two courtyards and a water garden. The striated space is dark and elegant, with black resin floors, fully glazed internal windows and concealed lighting designed to highlight the pattern of the cladding. A sunken cinema room provides a stratum of pure colour, while two guest bedrooms are also accessed off this long reception space. The master suite contains a dressing room, wet room and steam room. A long internal swimming pool runs alongside, and is painted in matt black to conjure the feeling of a cave.

The Lost House faces inward onto its own landscape, a space rich with chiaroscuro and intrigue, with bold colours in the bedrooms. Intended as a backdrop to fashion shows and receptions, it exploits its sunken, concealed location to create a space that appears to have been carved out of the geology of the cityscape.

1 From the street, the Lost House is deliberate ambiguous and invisible, giving no hint at what lies within.
2 Adjaye's brief was for a rich, complex interior, a space for entertaining and presentation, in keeping with the fashion industry lives of his clients. The striated walls and ceilings incorporate mirrors, lighting and texture, all reflected in the resin floors. An internal courtyard and pool brings light into the living room and further animates the reflections that shape the perception of the interior.

HIGHPOINT I AND II

London N6
Architect: *Berthold Lubetkin*
1935 and 1938

APARTMENT

Previous pages. Berthold Lubetkin, pictured in 1938 alongside the caryatid support pillar of Highpoint II.

The rear elevation of Highpoint I today. It is architecturally venerated and occupied by a coterie of like-minded tenants and owners, all of whom value the building and the community it has engendered.

1   The lobby of Highpoint II, a generous public/private space that demonstrated the more luxurious and well-appointed approach taken by the second building.

2   The public areas of Highpoint I are sparser but no less spatially intriguing, with expressive curves, glass bricks and circular columns presenting a compact summation of the modern aesthetic in a single space.

3–4 A typical Highpoint I apartment, with the ribbon window, unadorned surfaces and clean lines. The steel windows were provided by Williams and Williams of Chester.

1	3
2	
	4

If the Isokon Building was the ultimate British manifestation of modest urban living for the urbane modernist, Highpoint I, 1935, was their upscale equivalent: a classically proportioned apartment building for the progressive middle classes who weren't willing to sacrifice space for ideology. The building was commissioned by the industrialist Sigmund Gestetner, manager of the duplicating machine company set up by his father.

Originally intended to house company staff, Highpoint I was designed by Berthold Lubetkin with Tecton, and engineered by Ove Arup. Making extensive and innovative use of reinforced concrete, the building's plan is in the shape of two joined cruciform blocks, ensuring apartments have a variety of views across the communal gardens (complete with a swimming pool and tennis courts).

Gestetner's dream of high-quality flats for workers was quickly superseded, although Highgate residents were initially suspicious of the 'socialist' appearance of the stark white walls, absence of decoration and Bauhaus inspired cantilevered balconies. Private buyers were lured by the quality of the design—with its modern kitchens, elegant balconies, spacious grounds, shared roof terrace and facilities—ensuring that the later Highpoint II, 1938, was far more luxurious, containing around a quarter of Highpoint I's 64 apartments.

Both buildings became iconic for their form and elegance, quickly transcending their socially progressive aspirations. Lubetkin himself occupied the big penthouse atop Highpoint II, with its far-reaching views, barrel-vaulted ceiling and clear allusions to Corbusian ideals and aesthetics. Highpoint II also bears one of the earliest examples of postmodernism, in the form of the caryatids pressed into service as structural columns for the entrance canopy. Together, the two blocks form one of the finest groupings of modernist architecture in Europe.

COLOPHON

PICTURE CREDITS

Cover
Tim Crocker

Introduction
Beth Evans; Rachel Harman;
French + Tye

Town House
Slip House: Tim Crocker
James Melvin House: Tim Crocker
The Framehouse: French + Tye
Span Housing: French + Tye;
Archive images: Tony Ray-
Jones / RIBA Collections; John
Donat / RIBA Collections
Herringbone House: French + Tye
Laslett House: French + Tye
House in Highgate Cemetery:
Rachel Harman
Bailey/Hickey House: French + Tye
Doctor Rogers' House: Tim
Crocker; Archive image: Tony
Ray-Jones / RIBA Collections
Fog House: Tim Crocker
South Hill Park: French + Tye
Shoreditch Prototype House:
Helene Binet; French + Tye
Winter House: French + Tye;
Archive image: Tony Ray-
Jones / RIBA Collections

Conversion
Martello Tower Y: Edmund Sumner
Michael Craig-Martin
Studio: French + Tye
Shadow House: Dirk Lindner;
James Brittain; Albert Hill
The Reservoir: French + Tye
The Workshop: French + Tye
An Art Collector's Warehouse:
French + Tye

Country House
The Walled Garden: French + Tye
Farnley Hey: Tim Crocker;
Archive image: Architectural Press
Archive / RIBA Collections
Red Bridge House: Tim Crocker
Stratton Park: Tom Scott
Sea Lane House: Albert Hill;
Archive image: Architectural Press
Archive / RIBA Collections
The Long Barn: Matt Lincoln
High & Over: French + Tye
Long Wall, Surrey: French + Tye
Ochre Barn: Tim Crocker
Long Wall, Suffolk: Sue Barr
Eagle Rock: Andy Earl
Augustus John Studio: Rachel Harman;
Archive images: Architectural Press
Archive / RIBA Collections
Manor Way: French + Tye
Ahm House: Tim Crocker

Apartment
Isokon Building: French + Tye;
Archive image: RIBA Collections
Roof Garden Apartment: Andy Stagg
Provender Mill: Matt Lincoln
Barbican Estate: Neil Perry
Lost House: Lyndon Douglas
Highpoint I and II: French + Tye;
Archive image: RIBA Collections

pp 59, 85, 137
© Jason Evans

PUBLISHER
Artifice, 2015
First Edition
ISBN 978-1-908967-72-5

EDITORS
Jonathan Bell, Matt Gibberd &
Albert Hill

ART DIRECTION & DESIGN
Tom Watt & Matt Lowe for Field Projects

The Modern House is printed on
sustainably sourced paper.

themodernhouse.net